CHISELING THE EARTH

How Erosion Shapes the Land

R.V. FODOR

ENSLOW PUBLISHERS, INC.

Bloy St. & Ramsey Ave.
Box 777
Hillside, N.J. 07205
U.S.A.

P.O. Box 38
Aldershot
Hants GU12 6BP
U.K.

Library of Congress Cataloging in Publication Data:

Fodor, R.V.
   Chiseling the earth.

   Includes index.
   Summary: Explains how contours of the land are
sculptured by violent phenomena such as landslides, as well
as gradually eroded by chemical and mechanical weathering.
    1. Erosion. [1.Erosion] I.Title.
QE571.F64   1983   551.3'02   82-18227
ISBN 0-89490-074-9

Printed in the United States of America

10 9 8 7 6 5 4 3

CONTENTS

1

SELF-DESTRUCTION

When the spring of 1971 moved into the region of Saint-Jean-Vianney, Quebec, Canada, mild weather combined with the winter-frozen land to create a deadly formula. Warm temperatures thawed the ground, and the thick, clay-rich earth became moist and soft. Several April rainfalls followed and increased the soil moisture to far above its normal amount. The ground's ability to remain firm greatly weakened. By May 4, the water-soaked earth beneath Saint-Jean-Vianney could no longer support the town. It began to move.

The first sign of something amiss in Saint-Jean-Vianney came at 7:00 p.m. Two residents noticed that their dogs had become highly nervous, as though sensing some unseen activity. One man described his pet's unusual behavior as the same as it had been during thunderstorms. Elsewhere in the community, Mr. P. Blackburn observed peculiar behavior in his cows. The herd refused to return to its grazing land. Eventually, Blackburn gave up trying to send the cows off and let the animals enter the barn for the night.

At 10:30, Mrs. L. LaForge called a neighbor to report that

she had felt movement, as though an earthquake had disturbed her house. In addition, Mrs. LaForge said that she could see the nighttime lights of Chicoutimi, a nearby town. This was particularly strange because a small hill blocked the direct line of sight between her house and Chicoutimi. Had the hill suddenly disappeared, she wondered.

It was 11:00 p.m. when one of Quebec's greatest disasters began to strike in force. A bus driver, Mr. J. Girard, was one of the first people to realize it. He was on his regular nightly bus route around town, picking up the men who worked the midnight shift at the Aluminium Company of Canada plant in Arivida. His bus carried 18 passengers when he turned off Stanley Street to head onto Harvey Road and saw what looked like a gully in the surface of the gravel street. He slowed the bus to drive over it with care. But when his front wheels reached the gully, Girard saw no ground where his headlights shone.

The bus lodged on the edge of the sudden drop-off and Girard, frightened, ordered his passengers out the rear door. He was the last to flee the stranded bus, and he reported later that his escape had felt as though he were running wildly on moving stairs.

Reaching stable ground, Girard turned and saw the red lights on his bus dropping into the earth. He then rushed to warn sleeping residents about the growing hole that was swallowing up their town. He was able to alert one household but could not reach three others nearby before their houses sank vertically out of sight.

In the distance Girard spotted the lights of a car approaching town. With no way to warn the driver of the landslide taking place, he could only helplessly watch the car come closer along Harvey Road. He saw the headlights eventually dive into the black hole.

An aerial view of the huge semicircular scar photographed three years after the May 4, 1971, landslide at Saint-Jean-Vianney, Quebec, Canada. What buildings remained after the slide were later removed.

Canadian Forces

The hole grew larger with each second, swallowing house after house of sleeping people as the earth beneath Harvey Road crumbled. The houses plunged into a soupy pool of clay that began to move down the Petit Bras valley as a wall of mud 35 feet (11 meters) high. Flowing at 16 miles (26 kilometers) an hour, it entered the Rivere aux Vases and, 2 miles (3 kilometers) from Saint-Jean-Vianney, spilled into the Saguenay River.

Within five minutes, much of Saint-Jean-Vianney had vanished. The mass of moving earth that hauled the town away measured about 9 million cubic yards (7 million cubic meters), or enough to fill over six Empire State Buildings. The total surface area lost was 350,000 square yards (268,000 square meters), the size of seventy football fields.

The destructive landslide carried away 34 houses, one bus,

and numerous cars, and demolished a bridge 140 feet (43 meters) long. It took 31 people to their deaths. Two hours after its start, at 1:00 a.m. on May 5, the landslide and all it had carried were gone, having washed away in the Saguenay River.

This catastrophe in Quebec is a violent example of erosion, the earth's natural process that loosens soil and rock and carries them off. The slide illustrated the speed with which erosion can make great changes in the landscape—such as creating a 75-foot (23-meter) cliff where the center of Saint-Jean-Vianney once stood—simply by the pull of gravity. And it demonstrated the dangers of erosion to humankind, as seemingly stable land disintegrated beneath a town.

Unlike the sudden disaster at Saint-Jean-Vianney, however, most erosion is a long, steady process. And it uses more than gravity to move portions of the earth to transport elsewhere. Water, wind, and ice also operate on the earth's surface and shape the appearance of the land. All of these erosional agents work constantly at wearing down mountains and hillsides, carving valleys and canyons, and robbing agricultural lands of rich soil.

A home carried away in the 1971 landslide at Saint-Jean-Vianney, Quebec, Canada. The background shows the steep cliff that formed during the slide.

Canadian Forces

The slowness of most erosion makes it almost imperceptible. The outline of a mountain, for example, may look the same for thousands of years even though the rock is being worn down and hauled off by erosional agents. Photographs taken in the 1800s of certain areas compared to recent photographs of the same areas often show landscapes that appear nearly identical over a century's time.

But erosion is persistent. Geologists, the scientists who study the earth, know, for example, that mountains as high as the Rockies once occupied Michigan, Wisconsin, and Minnesota. Eroded over hundreds of millions of years, only "roots" of those early mountains remain today. And looking ahead, geologists know that erosion gradually will gnaw the majestic Rockies and the mighty Appalachians down to flat lands.

Farmers, too, understand that erosion is relentless. Many still lose fertile soil to wind and water even though they practice conservation by special plowing and planting techniques. And many shoreline residents fear that the waves of only one furious storm will steal the land from beneath their homes and wash it to sea.

The scar (light color) remains where part of a mountainside in Wyoming slid into the Gros Ventre River valley in 1925. *U.S. Geological Survey*

Although normally a slow, gradual process, erosion at times acts with force and swiftness greater even than that of the Saint-Jean-Vianney landslide. Mountainsides, for example, have tumbled into valleys in only minutes. In the famous Gros Ventre landslide in 1925, nearly 50 million cubic yards (38 million cubic meters) of rock roared 1½ miles (2½ kilometers) down a Wyoming mountainside within three minutes. And even faster erosion occurs when rocks break off cliffs and fall freely to the ground. Those events take only seconds.

The impact of erosion on humankind goes back in history to thousands of years before Christ. For instance, the ancient Babylonian society of the Middle East suffered erosion that continually washed soil into irrigation canals needed for agriculture. However, the Babylonians had to concentrate on fighting off invading tribes, so they had little time and manpower to improve the conditions of the canals. With poor irrigation, crops eventually failed and, in time, the Babylonian Empire withered too.

The ability of erosion to wear down mountains is clearly seen at the Badlands National Monument, South Dakota, where the vegetation cover is sparse.   *Soil Conservation Service*

Among the first to study erosion working on the earth's surface were early Greeks and Romans. One philosopher, Herodotus (485-435 B.C.), noted that the Nile River carried sediments, which are sand and clay, and dropped them at its mouth in the Mediterranean Sea. And Aristotle (394-322 B.C.) observed that all rivers removed rock fragments from land and transported them to sea. Sediments in the Black Sea, Aristotle commented, had washed in so rapidly over a sixty-year period that it became necessary to sail the sea in smaller boats.

Erosion by rivers such as the San Juan in Utah creates deep canyons and valleys.

U.S. Geological Survey

During the centuries after the fall of the Roman Empire, there was almost no scientific thinking about the earth. It was the sixteenth and seventeenth centuries before philosophers again gave attention to the earth and its erosional processes. During that time, people believed that the age of the earth was only 6000 years old, instead of the 4½ billion years it is now known to be. Accordingly, their observations of the earth's surface led them to conclude that the landscapes could only have been carved over such a short time by highly violent and catastrophic events, such as floods and earthquakes. This explanation for the different landforms became known as catastrophism.

True scientific examinations of erosional processes began in the mid-1700s with James Hutton, a Scottish physician who had strong interests in geology. Hutton remains most famous for his stand as a "Plutonist" against the group of scientists considered to be "Neptunists." As a Plutonist, Hutton correctly argued that the commonplace rock granite formed by cooling from molten material beneath the surface, rather than having originated in ancient seas as the Neptunists believed.

Hutton's greatest contribution to science was his recognition that "the present is the key to the past." This is the law of uniformitarianism. By presenting this principle, Hutton directly opposed the numerous scientists who supported catastrophism. He challenged catastrophism with a theory that the earth's surface changes by uniform, gradual processes over long spans of time.

Erosion is removing part of this Virginia housing development even before any occupants have moved in.   *Soil Conservation Service*

Hutton pointed out that the processes taking place every day, such as streams wearing down mountains, have always been active and will continue to be in the future. And he argued that stream erosion caused most of the landscape features.

But after Hutton's death, the Church resisted his views, and many scientists of the early 1800s were determined to explain the earth in terms of statements written in the Bible. They believed, for example, that the catastrophic Flood of Noah's time had carved the landscapes, particularly valleys.

By the mid-1800s, British geologist Charles Lyell was following in Hutton's footsteps, firmly opposing catastrophism. In his fight for uniformitarianism, Lyell used scientific measurements of the amounts of sediments carried by rivers to help prove that erosion is a constant process. He emphasized in his writings how certain landscapes, such as the regions around the Bay of Naples, Italy, and Glen Roy in the Scottish highlands, had changed by gradual uplifting or sinking. At Naples, for example, the Roman Temple of Jupiter Serapis had three tall columns with clam borings up to 23 feet (7 meters) above sea level. The Temple, Lyell concluded, had been submerged in seawater and re-elevated within the previous two thousand years, yet without undergoing any catastrophy. A violent event would have toppled the columns.

Homes built along shorelines can become victims of wave erosion.
Soil Conservation Service

Through such arguments, Lyell gradually convinced scientists that few landforms were the products of violent disturbances. He succeeded in bringing uniformitarianism to rule geologic thinking by the late 1800s.

In the early 1900s the scientific investigations of the American geologist and Harvard University professor William M. Davis provided a deeper understanding of erosion. Davis established the cycle of erosion, the theory that a landscape passes through a sequence of stages: youthful, mature, and old-age.

According to Davis, the youthful stage of erosion of a newly exposed surface (such as land recently uplifted from a sea floor) will have steep-walled, or V-shaped, valleys. Rapids and waterfalls may be present, and the stream valleys will be spaced far apart, separated by uplands, or "divides," that are flat and broad.

In a mature landscape, waterfalls and rapids are absent, and the streams meander, or wind, in wide valleys. Streams and tributaries have cut back into the uplands, and the divides are sharp and ridge-like. More and closer streams exist.

Old-age landscapes have extremely broad valleys, and the high areas separating the streams are nearly worn away.

There is no set time in which landscapes erode from youthful, to mature, and to old-age. How rapidly that erosion occurs in a particular area depends greatly on the climate and on the nature of the rock.

Climate in the form of the amount of rainfall and in temperature ranges acts to disintegrate rocks, or to break them down. This process is called weathering. Weathering does not always precede or assist erosion, but frequently it does. And the greater the weathering of rocks, the easier it is for water, wind, ice, and gravity to carry them off and to lower the level of the land.

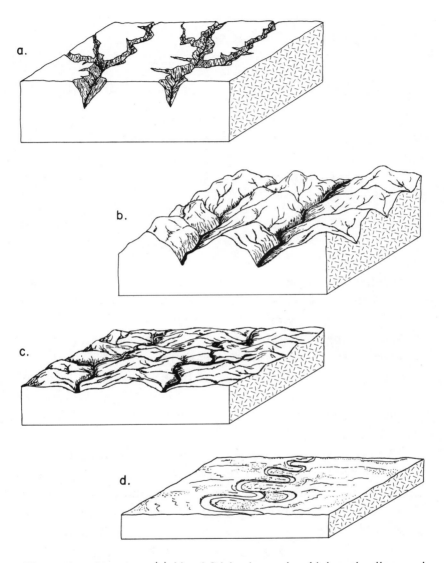

The cycle of erosion. (a) Youthful landscape has V-shaped valleys and broad, flat divides between the valleys. (b) Mature landscape has wider valleys and tributaries have greatly eroded the divides. (c) Landscape eroded to an advanced maturity state. (d) Old-age landscape, where the valleys are wide and flat, and the divides are almost worn down entirely.   *G.D.Garrett*

2

DISAPPEARING ROCKS: WEATHERING

Groundwater flowing beneath central Florida is slowly dissolving the rock below the surface. In places, the water has carved out large "rooms," or caverns, and weakened the overall strength of the underground rock layers. As long as groundwater remains in these caverns, however, there is little danger of their "roofs" collapsing. But if the groundwater were to suddenly disappear, the rock would lose supporting strength. The ground above might cave in. This happened at Winter Park, Florida, on May 8, 1981.

The growing population of Winter Park had been pumping out more and more groundwater for personal use. The subsurface level of the groundwater, called the water table, had therefore been steadily dropping. To make groundwater conditions worse, a drought, a long period with less than normal rainfall, hit central Florida in 1980. By early 1981, caverns below the surface had become empty of water.

The first trouble in Winter Park struck the Owens family. With little warning, the ground beneath their house and yard dropped nearly 100 feet (30 meters) into a huge circular hole.

Dissolved limestone collapsed beneath Winter Park, Florida, in May 1981, to form this large sinkhole.   *U.S. Geological Survey*

The crater that developed was 340 feet (100 meters) across, about the size of a football field. It was large enough to include several properties surrounding the Owens residence, such as parts of a four-lane road and a swimming pool, a parking lot, five cars, and a truck. Total losses from the damage reached two million dollars. And filling the sinkhole later would require spending money for 10,000 truckloads of dirt.

Cave-ins soon followed nearby as the sponge-like rock underlying Winter Park residential sections further collapsed. In all, nine sinkholes were carved into the Florida landscape that week. Land collapsing in central Florida, however, was not new or unexpected. Dozens of other similar cave-ins had already taken place in the region, some several thousands of years earlier.

Few areas across the world are similarly spotted with sinkholes. In the United States, only parts of Florida, Kentucky, Indiana, Tennessee, and Virginia have this type of landscape called karst. On the other hand, the geological process that creates karst lands takes place almost everywhere, producing various other effects. It is a form of rock decay called chemical weathering.

Rocks decay much the way a common nail does when it is left in the soil. A nail exposed long to air and moisture rusts and dissolves to a sliver of metal. Similarly, water and air attack the minerals that make up rocks. With enough time, some minerals dissolve as salt does in water. The engravings on tombstones made of the common rock limestone, for example, become washed out and illegible after exposure to humid climate for a century or two. And it is limestone that groundwater dissolves in karst regions such as Winter Park, and forms into the world's large caves and caverns such as Carlsbad Caverns in New Mexico and Mammoth Cave in Kentucky.

Limestone decays by a type of chemical weathering called

Karst landscapes have numerous sinkholes, as in this limestone-rich area of Puerto Rico.   *U.S. Geological Survey*

Cavities form in limestone as chemical weathering gradually dissolves it.
U.S. Geological Survey

Weathering by acid rain in Athens, Greece, has removed the details of the figures supporting the porch roof of the Erechtheum. *R. V. Fodor*

dissolution. It occurs because limestone is made of calcium carbonate, a substance that acid dissolves.

The acid in nature that attacks limestone is a weak variety formed when falling rain droplets acquire small amounts of carbon dioxide gas from the atmosphere. This mixture of water and carbon dioxide becomes the compound carbonic acid. Although it is mild, carbonic acid is capable of slowly dissolving limestone by breaking it into individual calcium and bicarbonate ions. To illustrate the chemical reaction between this acid and limestone, scientists use the chemical symbols:

$$CaCO_3 \quad + \quad H_2CO_3 \quad \rightarrow \quad Ca^{++} \quad + \quad 2HCO_3^-$$

| limestone | carbonic acid | calcium ion | bicarbonate ion |

Limestone, however, is seldom pure calcium carbonate, $CaCO_3$. While calcium carbonate is forming into limestone on the floors of the seas, clays mix in with it. Later, during weathering of the limestone on land, the clays within do not dissolve. Instead, dissolution leaves these sediments behind as loose particles that accumulate as soil.

Although carbonic acid decays rock, it is too weak to harm plants and animals. On the other hand, plant life changes the condition of the acid. As vegetation decays in soil, it provides additional carbon dioxide to the water seeping through the ground and increases the water's strength as an acid.

Industrial pollution, too, strengthens the acid that contacts rocks. Both automobile exhaust and gases emitted from industrial smokestacks create modern-day weathering problems. Rainwater rich in carbon dioxide and sulfur becomes "acid rain" and decays city monuments and buildings. Athens, Greece, has particularly serious weathering problems. The polluted atmosphere and acid rain of that city are disintegrating the priceless marble (also made of calcium carbonate) ruins of ancient Greece, such as the Parthenon. And in India, the Taj Mahal is undergoing flaking, pitting, and discoloring. Environmental experts worry that the strong industrial atmosphere attacking this marble mausoleum will destroy it within the next fifty years.

Chemical weathering affects all types of rock, but in different ways. Granite, for example, decays severely in moist climates because it contains a large amount of the mineral feldspar, which acidic water readily attacks. But unlike limestone weathering, feldspar does not dissolve. Rather, it is changed, or altered, to clay. The process is hydrolysis.

It occurs because water passing through microscopic spaces and cracks in granite removes, or leaches, certain components of the feldspar in the granite, such as the element potassium. The water carries them off and leaves behind a chemically different substance—a clay mineral. During this weathering process, the granite crumbles apart.

Chemical weathering, then, creates soil, one of man's most vital natural resources. Soil is made of rock fragments and minerals left from the decay of large bodies of rock.

But soil is formed by more processes than chemical

Photomicrograph showing the weathering of a feldspar crystal (1 cm long) in a volcanic rock. The outer portion has altered to a clay mineral, while some of the interior of the grain (lightest portion) remains fresh.   *R.V.Fodor*

As water freezes in cracks, it expands and exerts pressure to force the rock apart.   *G.D.Garrett*

weathering. Soil development is sometimes assisted by another type of weathering that breaks rocks apart, or fragments them. This is mechanical weathering, or physical weathering.

As with chemical weathering, water plays a major role in mechanical weathering. The reason is that when water freezes to ice, it increases slightly in volume. And while increasing in volume, freezing water exerts a powerful wedge-like force on whatever contains it. For instance, a glass jar full of water placed in a freezer may shatter as the water becomes ice.

In the same manner, water freezing and expanding within cracks in rocks exerts pressure to widen the cracks and further split the rocks apart. The forces of frost-wedging, as this process is called, are capable of lifting a block of rock the size of a small house.

Vegetation growing in rock fractures weathers rock in a similar way. Trees and tree roots that grow deep into cracks gradually force the rocks apart. A demonstration of the wedging power of trees is seen when the slabs of city sidewalks are uplifted by the roots of nearby trees.

For frost and plant wedging to begin, however, passageways for water must already exist in the rock. If the rock mass originated as sediment layers, or sediment "beds," that accumulated in ancient oceans, there may be fractures for groundwater to enter along the bedding planes of the rock. If the rock mass formed from the cooling of molten material, such as a lava flow, there may be fractures called joints. Rock shrinks, or contracts, slightly when cooling and the joints develop.

On the other hand, fractures can form in large bodies of rock because of expansion. As erosion carries off rock, it removes weight, or pressure, from the rock below. The rock below, then, may react like a smashed rubber ball that is relieved of the squeezing force. With pressure gone, it expands. The expansion of large rock bodies due to unloading of the upper portions can "spall," or fracture the rock into sheets.

Workers in marble quarries and in coal mines know of expansion "bursting." At times, when the workers are stripping rock from quarry and mine floors, the underlying rock has expanded and sheeted rapidly and explosively. Workers find themselves in "battlefields" of flying rock, and heavy mine equipment may be upset by the bursting rock.

Once mechanical weathering begins, additional water can enter for further frost-wedging. Also, with more fractures, chemical weathering can operate better to decay the rock because water can reach more rock surface.

Frost-wedging is sometimes aided by chemical weathering

As trees grow and increase in size, they can weather rock by wedging it apart.

Joints may form during the cooling of igneous rock in the earth's crust. These fractures allow water to enter, causing physical and chemical weathering.

The fractures in this rock quarry formed mainly by expansion, the release of overlying rock by erosion or quarrying.

U.S. Geological Survey

to create a type of mechanical weathering called exfoliation. This process causes large outcroppings of rock to sheet, or flake off, in a way that resembles the peeling of an onion. Sheeting to form rounded outcrops takes place because rainwater seeps into pore spaces and alters minerals to clay. As clay is formed, it absorbs water and expands to a volume larger than the mineral (such as feldspar) it replaces. This expansion, plus frost-wedging, provides the forces needed to spall curved rock-sheets off outcrops. Well-known exfoliation features include Stone Mountain, Georgia; Looking Glass Rock, North Carolina; and the domes of Yosemite National Park, California.

Exfoliation of the rock comprising Emeric Dome in Yosemite National Park, California.

U.S. Geological Survey

Spheroidal weathering occurs as shells of rock peel from boulders that are undergoing chemical and physical deterioration.

U.S. Geological Survey

Individual boulders decay in a variety of exfoliation called spheroidal weathering. Once the rounded shells of rock begin to peel away in onionskin fashion, the size of a boulder decreases steadily until the entire rock has become soil.

Forest fires and brushfires also mechanically weather rock by spalling. Fire heating a rock surface causes a thin outer layer to expand, split off, and drop away in a sheet. Also, forest fires that engulf boulders can heat them to a point where they split open.

Geologists once believed that sunshine warming a rock surface followed by nighttime cooling had the same weathering effects as heating rock by fire, only taking a much longer time. But laboratory tests on the heating and cooling of rocks failed to show any fragmentation caused by long periods of day-night temperature changes. In one experiment, scientists heated and cooled granite between the temperatures of 59 and 275 degrees Fahrenheit (15 and 135 degrees Celsius) every fifteen minutes.

By comparing the annual mean (average) temperature and annual mean rainfall of a region, the kind of weathering and its intensity can be estimated. *This diagram is based on the work of L. Peltier, published in the Assoc. Am. Geog., Ann., 40, p. 214-236; 1950.*   G.D.Garrett

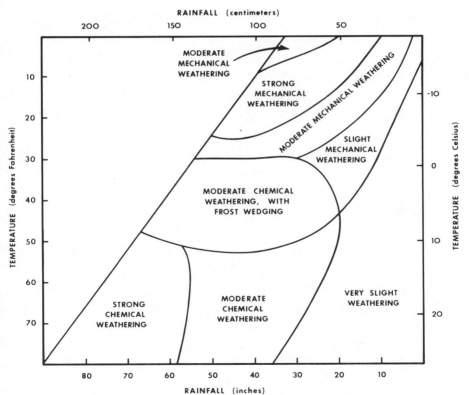

The test equaled 244 years of day-night heating and cooling, yet the granite showed no signs of disintegration.

Although chemical and mechanical weathering work hand-in-hand, one or the other type is usually more active in any particular region. Which one is more pronounced depends on the climatic factors of the region, mainly rainfall and temperature.

A moist climate favors chemical weathering. The landscapes receiving abundant rainfall, over 50 inches (125 centimeters) per year, undergo much more chemical decay than those receiving sparse rainfall. Accordingly, the wetter eastern United States has thicker and richer soil covers than the arid western states of Arizona, New Mexico, Nevada, and Utah.

On the other hand, large temperature changes over a 24-hour day in a cold climate promote mechanical weathering. A wide, daily temperature range passing above and below the freezing point results in repeated melting of ice and freezing of water trapped in rock fractures. Because daily temperatures in arid western states commonly change by 30 to 35 degrees Fahrenheit (17 to 20 degrees Celsius), and because rainfall is low, frost wedging is most effective there, forming rocky and angular landscapes.

Climate also determines how deep beneath the surface weathering takes place. The more rainfall an area receives, the more water is available to seep far below the surface and disintegrate rocks.

Both rock type and climate determine how rapidly weathering occurs. One study compares the weathering rates of granite and limestone in an arid region. The surfaces of granite statues carved by early Egyptians decayed in the desert 1 to 2 millimeters per thousand years, while limestone making up the pyramids weathered as fast as 1 centimeter in only fifty years.

Moist climates take their toll of granite, however. In 1880, two granite obelisks, each known as a Cleopatra's Needle, were moved to humid environments from the Egyptian desert where they had been standing for 3500 years. One was placed in London, the other in Central Park, New York. At the time of their transfers, little weathering was noticeable, and the deeply cut hieroglyphs on the obelisks were clear and sharp.

In their new climates, frost, water, and air that is rich in industrial carbon dioxide quickly attacked the granite. Weathering reduced the legibility of the hieroglyphs in the

The carvings on this Egyptian obelisk lost clarity and sharpness due to weathering in less than 40 years in New York City. This photograph was taken in 1918.

Metropolitan Museum of Art

obelisks and rounded the sharp corners. One scientist estimates that more weathering of the granite obelisk occurred in Central Park in only one hundred years than had taken place during two thousand years in Egypt.

Through their studies and observations, scientists know generally that weathering is slowest in the hot, dry climates of deserts. It is fastest in the hot, moist climates of tropical jungles.

But if weathering requires moisture and atmosphere, the surface of the moon must have weathered differently. The moon has no water or atmosphere, yet the Apollo Space

There is no water or atmosphere on the moon, but weathering has occurred by the repeated bombardment of its surface by meteorites.

National Aeronautics and Space Administration

Program photographs and the visits by Apollo astronauts showed that the moon has a thick gravelly cover of rock chips and dust.

The explanation is that the moon's original rock surface has been pulverized by the bombardment of meteorites, rocks moving through space. Over its 4½ billion years of existence, millions of meteorites have impacted the moon and have mechanically weathered its surface. Meteorites fall to earth, too, but the atmosphere offers protection. Most space material attracted to earth burns up in the atmosphere before reaching the surface.

3

MOVING MOUNTAINS

When construction of the Vaiont Dam began in the Italian Alps in the 1950s, some of the project engineers noticed certain geologic features at the damsite that could be hazards once the dam was completed. First, the rock type was largely limestone, which is easily decayed by chemical weathering. Second, the mountainsides that would contain the reservoir behind the dam had "rebound" joints, large fractures formed during earlier erosion and unloading of overlying rock. Third, during excavations and tunneling at the damsite, rock bursts and sheeting occurred. Finally, the damsite showed evidence of ancient landslides. All of these features pointed to a threat of new landslides once the dam was completed and held a deep reservoir of water behind it.

But enough engineers believed that the danger of future landslides was not great and that modern engineering techniques could prevent slides. Construction continued and the Vaiont Dam was completed in the fall of 1960.

Shortly afterwards, engineers working at the new dam detected that portions of the mountainsides forming the

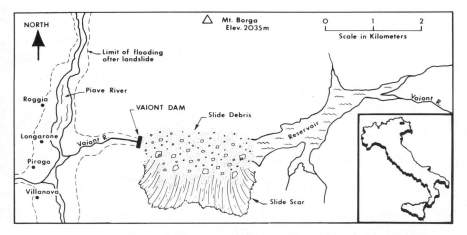

A location map for the Vaiont landslide of 1963. Rock on the wall of the reservoir behind the dam slipped into the reservoir, splashing water over the dam to flood the region and towns below.   *G.D.Garrett*

reservoir walls were creeping, or slowly sliding downward. Movements of several inches a week sometimes occurred, but more commonly the reservoir walls crept less than an inch (about 1 centimeter) per week. Still, no one expressed concern about a possible disastrous landslide. Any slides, the engineers felt, would be small. They had no idea that a monstrous slab of rock 1½ miles (2½ kilometers) long and 1 mile (1½ kilometers) wide was about to slip off the mountain wall.

Beginning mid-September 1963, measuring stations around the reservoir recorded sudden increases in rock creep, up to 1 centimeter a day. At the end of September, heavy rains began and continued almost steadily for nearly two weeks. Locations around the reservoir began creeping at rates of 20, 30, and 40 centimeters a day.

Finally, on October 8 engineers realized that a true danger existed. Fearful now that a mountainside would plunge into the reservoir and send the water up and over the dam, they began to lower the water level behind the dam. But their actions were too late.

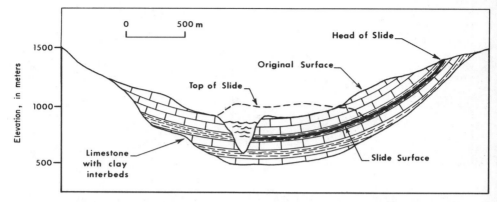

A simplified geologic cross section at the Vaiont Dam illustrating how the wall slid along a weak and "lubricated" plane (the heavy line).

G.D.Garrett

On the rainy night of October 9, 312 million cubic yards (240 million cubic meters) of water-soaked mountainside, mostly rock, tore off and plummeted into the reservoir at a speed of nearly 100 feet (30 meters) per second. Water in the reservoir splashed out as a wall 300 feet (90 meters) higher than the dam. Within minutes a raging flood roared down the valley below the dam and wiped out all life and buildings for miles beyond, including the towns of Longarone, Pirago, and Villanova. In all, the torrent claimed nearly 3000 lives.

The Vaiont disaster, like the Saint-Jean-Vianney catastrophe, was caused by erosion moving large masses of earth in a short period of time. Geologists refer to such great events as a mass movement, or a mass wasting, of land. "Landslide," however, is the commonly used name.

Although gravity brings landslides down, there are certain other geologic conditions necessary for slides to occur. At Vaiont, for example, the landslide was related to the geologic strength and structure of the rock forming the mountainside above the reservoir. It had bedding planes dipping into the reservoir. Geologists view bedding planes as zones of weakness in layers of rocks that enable the layers to slide along each other like cards in a deck. In addition, the limestone at Vaiont contains seams of clay which behaved as "slip planes." And finally, groundwater had long been weakening the limestone at the damsite. The Vaiont region, therefore, was a poor site on which to construct a dam and reservoir.

Anywhere rock layers dip down a mountainside into a valley a landslide is possible. The pull of gravity is always present, and a slide may be awaiting a particular outside event to trigger it. This may be a rain-soaking or a deep undercutting of the mountainside by a river, which may reduce the support for the dipping rock. These were the conditions preceding the gigantic Gros Ventre slide. Near Yellowstone National Park, the Gros Ventre River had carved a channel at the base of Sheep Mountain and removed the support for a thick slab of dipping sandstone. Only friction between the sandstone and an under-

Steeply dipping beds such as these along a Colorado highway can slide apart like cards in a deck.   *U.S. Geological Survey*

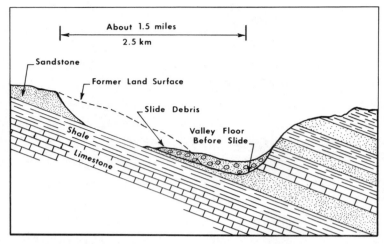

A simplified geologic cross section illustrating how the steeply dipping beds that were undercut by the Gros Ventre River (shown as the valley floor) enabled a Wyoming mountainside to fail in 1925.

G.D.Garrett

lying layer of soft shale (a clay-rich rock) kept the sandstone layer in place. It held until melting winter snows and heavy rains in the spring of 1925 lubricated the shale layer and reduced its friction "grip" on the sandstone. The amount of rock that eventually ripped from the mountain and spilled into the valley was enough to fill a train of railroad hopper-cars stretching from California to New York.

The energy of the Gros Ventre slide was so great that the nose of the slide flowed across the valley and up the opposite wall 300 feet (90 meters). When the debris finally settled in the valley as the largest landslide in United States history, it created an enormous dam that remains across the Gros Ventre River today.

Sometimes man is the trigger for giant landslides, as at Elm, Switzerland. Curiously, this disaster has its origin with the introduction of compulsory education in Europe in the nineteenth century. Attending the sudden growth of public

This rockslide poured out of a mountain in Switzerland as a "tongue" of debris.

Swissair

schools during that time was a demand for slate to use as classroom chalkboard. Business-minded Elm residents who knew that they could make money by mining and selling slate set up a slate-quarry operation. Some of the men—none with mining or quarrying experience—began extracting slate from a seam in a nearby mountain.

They successfully excavated large quantities of slate, but when they were working nearly 165 feet (50 meters) into the mountainside, trouble began. A large crack developed and millions of tons of rock above the quarry began to creep downward. Stones tumbled off the sliding rock mass almost continually, injuring workers and eventually forcing the closing of the quarrying operation.

Worried now about a landslide, Elm villagers summoned professional advice. However, when a consultant arrived from their capital city, he advised the people merely to remove the weight of fallen trees from the sliding areas. The next day, September 10, 1881, the mountain rumbled down at 100 miles

Cones of talus, or fallen rock, forming at the base of Sheep Rock Mountain, Oregon.

(160 kilometers) an hour, burying the hamlet of Untertal and part of Elm, killing 155 persons.

A mass movement of great rock slabs that are sliced off mountainsides, breaking into boulders on the way down, is more accurately called a rockslide, a rock avalanche, or a rock fall, rather than a landslide. The term avalanche, however, is shared with giant walls of snow and ice that break loose and spill down from mountains. And rock falls may be lesser erosional events, such as the occasional tumbling of boulders from a cliff face. The debris that collects at the cliff bottom is called talus.

"Quick clay" can both support weight (the core of clay holds 11 kilograms) and pour like watery mud. The change from solid to liquid usually happens suddenly, such as from the rapid addition of water or from earthquake shock.

National Research Council of Canada

Unlike the Vaiont, Gros Ventre, and Elm mass movements, the ground that crumbled beneath Saint-Jean-Vianney was practically free of rock. Geologically, it was made of material able to change from solid soil to "soupy" soil in only minutes. Scientists call this type of earth "quick clay."

The particles making up quick clay are mostly flakes of clay minerals smaller than a pin-point. They are bonded by electrostatic forces and by water trapped in the pores between the flakes. Normally, quick clay is rigid and can support overlying weight such as buildings as well as other soils. But a heavy rain-soaking may burden quick clay with added weight and disrupt the network of particles so that the clay suddenly collapses like a house built of cards. Water in the pores breaks free and the clay becomes a watery mud. This is how the Saint Jean-Vianney landslide became a mudflow that washed 2 miles (3 kilometers) down a valley to finally spill into the Saguenay River.

Most often, however, a mudflow and similar types of landslides known as debris flow and earthflow are movements of ordinary soil and clay, rather than failing quick clay. Each of these flows commonly begins where hillsides slump under the weight of excessive rainwater or too much housing construction. A debris flow contains abundant rock fragments as well as mud and sand, whereas earthflows and mudflows are composed largely of mud and sand. A mudflow is the most liquid of the three types, able to move down valleys like wet concrete. All of these flows are sometimes referred to by the casual name of mudslide.

Mudslides have long been destructive in California, where thousands of residents live in homes built on hillsides. Nearly every year rains drench some part of California and bring hillsides alive, slumping or flowing like molasses. Sliding houses crash into neighboring ones, and mud streams through and over those houses that manage to remain standing. Each mudslide costs millions of dollars in property damage and may, in addition, claim several lives.

Many California landslides have occurred in residential areas that became rain-soaked, as at Laguna Beach in 1978.   *GeoPhoto*

A car, garage, and boulders transported by a debris flow, Los Angeles
County, California.   *U.S. Geological Survey*

Where a hillside breaks loose as a landslide but does not
flow, the movement is called slump. A slump block has a curved
backside, as though it was scooped out with a giant spoon.
Some slump blocks, however, partly become flows
when their lower portions are water-logged and spread out and
away from the bottom of the block.

Where debris flows and earthflows spill into streams, they
may change the streams into mudflows. This happened after

Mount Saint Helens' volcanic eruption in Washington State on May 18, 1980. Heat from the eruption melted snow and ice on the volcano's flanks, and the meltwater washed enormous amounts of rocky debris down the volcano and into nearby rivers. Walls of volcanic ash, mud, and rocks oozed at 30 miles (48 kilometers) an hour down nearby rivers such as the Toutle that day, killing motorists, snapping trees and highway bridges, and sweeping away homes and logging equipment.

The Toutle River in Washington State turned into a mudflow after the Mount Saint Helens volcanic eruption in May 1980.

U.S. Geological Survey

A close-up view of the slump blocks along the South Nation River, Ontario, Canada. *National Research Council of Canada*

Earth swollen with water or made of quick clay may remain stable until disturbed by outside movement, such as the shaking of an earthquake. In Alaska, for example, the powerful Good Friday earthquake of March 27, 1964, set off dozens of landslides. Many occurred in uninhabited areas and were noticed only because they fell onto glaciers. The piles of dark rocks like the avalanche that fell onto Sherman Glacier were sharply visible from the air against the bright underlying ice.

In contrast, the 1964 earthquake triggered damaging erosion at populated Anchorage, Alaska. The main reason was that this city lies on a thick layer of clay. Part of the damage that occurred while Anchorage was shaking from the earthquake happened because a water-rich zone of clay below Turnagain Heights weakened and sheared. Suddenly a slab of ground tens of feet thick and with a wet and lubricated base was disconnected and free to move.

Gravity quickly took over and pulled the slab of clay down a gentle slope toward the Cook Inlet waterway, moving it like a block of ice cream sliding across a countertop. Fractures formed and widened near the back of the slide, and the houses and buildings overlying the cracks slumped with the crumbling earth and split open. The main portion of the Turnagain Heights land-slide moved for nearly five minutes, including one minute of slipping after the earthquake vibrations had stopped. When the slide block came to rest, its toe was a buckled-up mound of

The great Alaskan earthquake of 1964 triggered a rock slide that blanketed the Sherman Glacier.   *U.S. Geological Survey*

Slumping in Anchorage, Alaska, triggered by the powerful March 1964
earthquake.   *U.S. Geological Survey*

debris on the mudflats on the inlet, nearly one-half mile (one
kilometer) from where it began.

Earthquakes set off submarine landslides too, most of which
go unnoticed. One that was both detected and timed moving was
a monstrous undersea collapse of the continental slope off the
Newfoundland, Canada, coast in 1929. The circumstances were
unusual because the underwater slide sent a murky, sediment-
laden current ripping across communication cables as it raced
along the sloping seafloor 375 miles (600 kilometers) toward
the deep ocean. Because it snapped the cables one after the
other, the times that the slide, or density current, passed various
points were determined electrically. It moved at speeds up to
65 feet (20 meters) a second.

When earthquakes, rain soakings, and undercutting of mountainsides are not triggering erosion, gravity is constantly eroding sloping landscapes everywhere by creep. This is the slowest form of mass movement, the gradual downward movement of surface rock and soil. Because of its slowness, however, creep can usually be detected only by noting man-made objects, such as fences and telephone poles. They become tilted as creep drags them downslope with the soil that they are fixed in.

Creep caused by gravity bringing down both soil and rock on this Maryland hillside.   *U.S. Geological Survey*

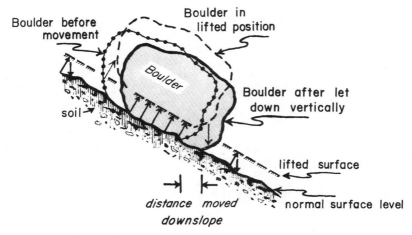

Alternating freezing and thawing of water heaves up soil particles and rocks enabling them to creep down hillsides in zig-zag fashion.

In addition to gravity, the greatest reason for creep is frost heaving. When moisture in the topsoil freezes and expands, it pushes up, or heaves, soil fragments. They rise perpendicular to the slope of hillside. When the ground thaws and dries, the particles settle. But because the particles fall vertically, they end up slightly downhill from their original positions. Repeated freezing and thawing causes soil and rock to go downslope in a series of these up-and-down, zig-zag movements.

The combination of mass movement and chemical and mechanical weathering works to shape all parts of the earth's surface. These geological processes sculpture landforms as widely different as the steep cliffs of arid regions and the gently rolling forest lands of humid regions.

But mass movement and weathering are only part of the erosional process. Additional chiseling of the earth takes place by the agents that carry loose material away: rivers, winds, oceans, and glaciers.

4

HAULING IT AWAY

The water on the earth's surface is part of an enormous recycling operation run by the sun's heat and the pull of gravity. Solar heat begins the hydrologic cycle, as it is called, by evaporating water from the oceans, the earth's main reservoir for water. It claims enough water to lower the level of the sea 3 feet (1 meter) every year. If water did not return to the seas, all ocean basins would dry up in about 4000 years.

Evaporated water in the atmosphere forms clouds of moisture that pass over the sea and land and eventually precipitate as rain and snow. Once on land, water takes a variety of paths. The greatest portion goes upward, evaporating into the atmosphere once again. Some water seeps into the soil to become groundwater, and vegetation collects and uses some water.

The most visible path of water, however, is its direct return to the sea as streams and rivers. Flowing under gravity's pull, running water entering oceans completes the hydrologic cycle. Along the way, it causes the most common and destructive form of erosion.

Stream erosion begins with raindrops hammering on soil. Each drop behaves like a miniature bomb, loosening and "exploding" soil particles outward from where the drop strikes. The raindrops of a single storm hitting a plot of land the size of a football field may disrupt and scatter 100 tons of soil.

The erosive force of a single raindrop is shown by its ability to carve a pit, or crater, when falling onto soil.

Navy Department

9,296

A sheet of rainwater moving across North Carolina farmland, taking fertile soil with it.   *Soil Conservation Service*

During heavy storms, rainwater running off a slope collects into sheets that capture and strip away loosened soil. As the sheetwash meets irregularities on the surface, however, it separates into channels of swiftly moving water. This rushing water may eventually carve its channels into rills and gullies, eroding still deeper soil, plus plant matter and nutrients, and wash them all into nearby creeks and streams. Left behind is fresh rock to weather and erode in future runoffs. With time, then, erosion from rainfall and runoff cuts hillsides and mountains down to flat lands.

Removal of vegetation to prepare farmland makes the soil an easy target for erosion by rainwater.   *Soil Conservation Service*

The people who suffer most from the robbery of soil by runoff are those who make their livings from the soil—the agriculturists. Curiously, they assist this kind of erosion. Whenever farmers clear vegetation from the surface to prepare for planting, they remove the protection of soil from raindrops and the plant roots that help keep soil compacted. Moreover, their plowing and tilling loosens soil and makes it easier for runoff to wash it away.

Soil scientists estimate that a football field-sized section of agricultural land loses 5 to 50 tons of soil to runoff every year. Much larger losses sometimes occur, such as the 250 tons of soil (per football-field size) recorded as having been washed off southwestern Iowa farmlands during only one 1950 raging downpour.

Nationwide, runoff claims about 3 billion tons of agricultural land every year. Of all the sediments presently in the world's rivers and streams, nearly half has been washed in from agricultural lands.

Runoff from pastures and forests and from mass movements such as rockfalls, mudslides, and creep account for most of the remaining sediments in running water. However, flowing water also acquires sediments by eroding its own channel bottom and walls. A river rounding a bend, for example, gnaws its outer bank, while water passing over a muddy or sandy river-bottom plucks and lifts the particles to carry them farther downstream.

Stream-bed erosion is most active during floods. The amounts and velocities of the water then are greater than normal. Within only hours, torrents may scour soft channels several feet deeper and flush away river banks and the buildings and vegetation on them. In the Big Thompson River flashflood, roaring water washed 230 buildings and 400 automobiles from Colorado's mountains and killed 139 people in the early morning hours of August 3, 1976. While deepening and widening its channel during the rampage, the flooding Big Thompson eroded sediments known to have been part of the river's bank for 7000 years.

The erosive powers of the flooding Big Thompson River, Colorado, washed away river banks and buildings on them in 1976.

Army Corps of Engineers, Omaha District

Streams use bedloads to erode channels made of hard rock. A bedload is composed of cobbles, pebbles, and sand—the sediments too large to remain suspended and transported in the water currents. By sliding and rolling and by bouncing across the stream bottom in a movement called saltation, bedload has the same effect as sandpaper dragged over wood. The rock fragments scrape and chip the stream floors to wear them away by abrasion. With time, bedloads can carve steep-walled gorges and canyons hundreds of feet deep.

As bedload particles abrade and down-cut stream channels, the cobbles and pebbles themselves wear away by striking one another. Corners and edges are chipped off, the pebbles becoming rounded and smooth as they decrease in size. Small dust-sized particles produced from clashing bedload remain in the water currents. This suspended load, too, can abrade as where the swirling currents carve potholes in the rock channel of a stream.

Rock polished and carved with potholes by the abrasive waters of the James River, Virginia.   *U.S. Geological Survey*

Alluvial fans building up at the foot of the Panamint Range, Death Valley, California.   *U.S. Geological Survey*

A stream continues to move its load and use it for eroding as long as its velocity is great enough. But where velocity decreases sharply, as where a stream emerges from mountains onto a gently-sloped valley floor, the water drops much of its load. The sediment piles up at the foot of the mountains to form an alluvial fan.

The sediment dropped where the Nile River spills into the Mediterranean Sea builds a delta (mainly the dark-colored area).

National Aeronautics and Space Administration

Water alone also can erode rock. The impact of water hammering rocks at the foot of a waterfall scours, polishes, and dissolves them. At Niagara Falls, for instance, plunging water constantly beats the soft shale rock near the base. As the shale erodes, the upper cliff of hard limestone loses support and eventually breaks off. The lip of the main part of the Falls erodes back this way about 3 feet (1 meter) each year. Occasionally it erodes catastrophically. One example occurred in 1954 when a block of limestone the size of the Lincoln Memorial in Washington, D.C., cracked off, tumbled into the 50-mile (80-kilometer)-per-hour cascade, and crashed at the bottom.

The depth to which a stream carves its valley or canyon is limited by base level. This is the elevation, or the height above sea level, of the body of water that the stream empties into. Sea level marks the ultimate base level. The reason is that a river, such as the Mississippi, cannot possibly erode its channel below sea level and then rise to spill into the sea, the Gulf of Mexico. Inland, any river or lake that running water enters is a "local" base level for that running water.

As rivers mix with the lakes or seas they enter, they drop their sand and clay loads. Waves capture the sediments and gradually move them along the shoreline away from the river mouth. The loads of rivers become the sands of beaches.

Some rivers supply more sediment than lake or sea waves can readily haul off. The excess material then accumulates and "fans" out from the river's mouth as a delta. For instance, the 500 million tons of debris that the Mississippi River carries to the Gulf of Mexico each year is more than the Gulf can distribute quickly. Much of the sediment therefore becomes part of the vast Mississippi delta in Louisiana, a feature equal in size to Massachusetts and Connecticut combined. The Mississippi River collects its enormous load from erosion by runoff, mass wasting, and stream action in 25 states.

Once sand grains are at a shoreline, waves may use them to erode by abrasion. Tossed against shoreline cliffs, rock particles in waves scrape and scour the sea walls. They carve out sea notches and caves and sometimes sculpture a cliff down to only pillars. These features are called sea stacks. As the cliffs erode, the waves use the rock fragments to further chisel away the cliffs.

Most erosion along shorelines, however, is from the motion of the water alone: the never-ending wave action. About 8000 waves roll onto a beach every day (24 hours). Their motion

These sea stacks are remnants of a rocky Oregon coastline attacked by wave erosion.

Oregon State Highway

shifts the beach grains along the shoreline. This happens because waves roll ashore at an angle to the shoreline (rather than parallel to it), whereby they move grains along the shore in zig-zag paths. When a wave washes in, sand grains roll up the beach at an angle to the shoreline—ZIG. The backwash of water that follows pulls the grains down the beach—ZAG. By day's end, waves may have transported particular grains hundreds of feet farther down a beach from where they began the day. They will have moved along shore by what is called the longshore current.

Waves rolling ashore at an angle push sand grains along the beach in a zig-zag manner. The general direction of water movement is called the longshore current.

Army Corps of Engineers, Wilmington, NC District

Accordingly, beaches are landforms in constant motion, changing shapes and sizes under the erosive power of waves. The constant attack from waves may reshape a beach in only tens of years. Comparisons between the detailed maps used by early adventurers along the Eastern Seaboard and the modern maps of the U.S. Geological Survey show that pirates sailed different coastlines. Over the decades, islands have changed in outline and size, and offshore sand bars have come and gone. Capes of land have grown larger or disappeared, while inlets have appeared and vanished. Because of waves and longshore currents, then, there is no assurance that the land beneath today's beachside towns, boardwalks, and resort motels will be high and dry in the next century.

As residents of seashore communities such as Cape May, New Jersey, have learned, however, shoreline erosion is more than beach sands shifting day-to-day with a longshore current. Cape May began in the eighteenth century as the nation's finest

Wave action constantly attacks shorelines, making beaches unreliable places on which to build.   *North Carolina Archives and History*

With each new storm, more of Cape May, New Jersey, crumbles into
the sea.   *Army Corps of Engineers, Philadelphia District*

beachside resort. Wealthy businessmen and politicians, including
presidents Pierce, Lincoln, and Grant regularly visited Cape May
for dinners and parties and for vacations on its broad beaches.
In 1908, Henry Ford displayed his latest model automobiles on
the firm sand of the beach.

Because the town of Cape May was separated from its
shoreline by hundreds of feet of sand dunes, residents felt safely
removed from the strongest waves that any storm could
possibly churn up. But security was not permanent. Over the
years that the town was growing in size and popularity, the sea
was slowly rising and encroaching on it. Even as early as 1859,
two shoreline lighthouses had tumbled into the ocean as rising
sea level undermined the beach beneath them.

It was the 1920s before Cape May residents became deeply
concerned about losing their seashore. More than 20 feet (6
meters) of beach were disappearing beneath the Atlantic Ocean
in some years. One of the runways of the airfield gradually was
crumbling into the sea, and a third lighthouse seemed certain to

The grassy dunes along this North Carolina shore have been gouged by high-energy storm waves.   *North Carolina State University Seagrant*

spill into the sea as the others had. The only protection for Cape May was to build walls against the seas and to haul new sand in to build up the beach.

But the sea kept rising, destroying the sea walls and robbing the beach sands. By 1962, the thin strip of beach that remained between the town and the ocean offered little protection from the raging storm that struck. Waves easily roared over the walls to flood the town. Repairs were later made on the walls, but the work has never ended. Cape May is a resort town in constant battle with seaside erosion determined to consume it with rising waters.

Cape May is not alone in having the sea nipping ever closer to erode new land. Towns all along the Atlantic coast are in similar danger from rising sea level. Properties at stake range from beachside summer homes, to irreplaceable seaside monuments like historic Cape Hatteras lighthouse in North Carolina, to luxurious Miami Beach hotels.

The erosional problem of rising seas is brought on by a slow warming of the world climate that is melting ice at the North and South Poles. The meltwaters increase the amount of water already in the ocean basins.

Because climatic changes are not constant, however, the rise in sea level has not been steady over the past few thousands of years. The long-term trend of sea level is upward, but geologists and oceanographers have determined that the rise may be as much as 3 feet (1 meter) over one century, and far less other times, only 1 foot (30½ centimeters) a century. Also, the changes in sea level are not the same everywhere. The reason is that coastlines may be rising or lowering, too. In Texas, for example, coastal land is sinking because of the rapid withdrawal of groundwater for industrial and residential purposes. But along the Baltic Sea and the Scandanavian coasts, land is rising about 1 centimeter each year due to upward movements in the earth's crust.

A growing sand dune along North Carolina's Outer Banks shoreline.
Tourist Bureau, Dare County

The significance of rising sea level is that an increase of only 2 inches (5 centimeters) brings water far inland. This is because many coastal regions are nearly flat landscapes. As an example, calculations for Nags Head, North Carolina, show that over the past century rising water has forced back the shoreline about 6 feet (2 meters) a year. And rising seas could put Galveston County, Texas, underwater by the year 2000.

Hurricane and tropical-storm waves cause the most rapid and devastating shoreline erosion. Storm waves striking beaches strip them of sand and wash away buildings and the land beneath them. At Gulfport, Mississippi, in 1969, Hurricane Camille's winds of 210 miles (335 kilometers) per hour sent sledgehammer-like waves ashore with the force to demolish a brick beachside motel and push three huge freighters onto the beach. History's most powerful storm waters include those stirred up by the hurricane that blasted through Galveston, Texas, in 1900. Erosive waters washed away over 3000 homes and buildings and more than 6000 people in them.

In many coastal areas, sand ridges at the tops of beaches protect the inland from storm waves. These dunes receive the full force of storms and usually, therefore, show the greatest effects of beach erosion. Hurricane Eloise's storm waves in 1975 swept inland 17 feet (5 meters) higher than the normal seaside water level and deeply gouged the dune ridge along Florida's panhandle. In less than one hour the waves chewed back the sand ridge more than 50 feet (15 meters). Dune retreat, as this erosion is called, leaves the seaward side of ridges as steep wave-cut cliffs.

Winds blowing in off the water eventually repair the dunes, however. Moving up a beach, winds push and carry small particles from the beach face and drop them at the top of the beach, building and rebuilding dunes.

An awesome dust storm blowing across the Midwest during the great Dust Bowl years, the 1930s, brings midnight to this Colorado farmland in midday.   *Soil Conservation Service*

The ability of wind to shift and carry grains makes it a strong erosional agent. This was demonstrated well in the 1930s when winds turned the southern Great Plains into the Dust Bowl.

The history of the Dust Bowl dates to the last part of the nineteenth century, when great numbers of settlers claimed land for farming in the southern Great Plains (parts of Oklahoma, Kansas, Colorado, New Mexico, and Texas). They found the land covered with an extensive blanket of grass, even though little rain had ever fallen on the region—only about 20 inches (50 centimeters) a year. Yet the weather and soil were suitable for making a living by farming crops, mainly wheat. In short time, the ambitious settlers had plowed the soil and planted crops on millions of acres of prairie land. They were unconcerned about the protection that the grasses had long given the soil against erosive winds and rain. Their chief interest

The dust storms of the 1930s left much of the land impossible to farm. The photograph of this abandoned farm was taken in 1937.

Soil Conservation Service

was to supply their families with food and to make money from the land.

A continuous flow of new people moved into the region through the early part of the twentieth century. Many used newly available gasoline-powered tractors for farming, and by 1930, few prairie-land acres had not been turned over and stripped of their grassy cover. The farming remained successful until peculiar weather conditions fell upon the overworked land. In 1931, a major drought withered crops and dried the soil to dust. Then the winds took over to rule for the following decade.

With only dust and no vegetation on the surface, winds easily gathered up the soil. They swirled it thousands of meters into the air and swept it across the country as great brown, black, and gray clouds that blotted out the sun. Dust polluted the air, and people and animals suffered from dust inhalation and eye infections. The dust damaged buildings, roads, railroads, shrubs, and trees. Much of it fell on Eastern states. Soil from Oklahoma and Kansas often ended up sprinkling cities as far away as Chicago, Atlanta, New York, and Boston.

Every year from 1931 to 1940, dozens of dust storms hauled off the soil that farmers had plowed years earlier. A record number of 72 large storms occurred in 1937, many of which moved across the plains at 60 miles (95 kilometers) an hour. One storm would sometimes blow out 5 million acres of soil, or more than twice the amount of earth removed to make the Panama Canal. Measurements determined that during a storm the air above a square mile of Great Plains could contain over 1000 tons of dust.

The most serious erosion during the Dust Bowl years was deflation of the land, the wind removing loose soil and leaving behind a scooped-out area. Although less of a problem in the Great Plains today because of better weather conditions and better farming techniques, deflation is active where little vegetation and rainfall occur, as in deserts. In some deserts, winds remove sand and dust from a place and leave a desert "pavement" of pebbles and cobbles behind. Or, if rocks are not part of the desert soil, the wind simply carves a blowout, a shallow depression in the landscape.

Grains too large for wind to pick up and carry are moved by saltation, the rolling and bouncing of grains and the hitting of others to set them into motion. Where wind and sand are abundant, abrasion by saltation is effective. However, as indicated by erosional marks on fence posts and telephone poles, saltation is restricted to within about 20 inches (½ meter) of the surface. Desert rocks sometimes acquire a polish from wind abrasion. Such a wind-smoothed cobble or boulder is called a ventifact.

Where rocks and vegetation are sparse, strong winds can "blow out" an area by removing the small soil particles. Comparison between the man and tree base in this Michigan scene shows how deeply the wind has carved.

Soil Conservation Service

A "pavement" formed of cobbles and pebbles on the desert floor at Death Valley National Monument, California. Winds have blown away the smallest particles.

U.S. Geological Survey

A large wind-polished boulder, or ventifact, in Sweetwater County, Wyoming.   *U.S. Geological Survey*

Winds drop the sediments that they transport wherever they slow down or meet an obstacle. If winds regularly unload in a particular area, the material accumulates and grows into dunes. This may be in a desert, but also, as has been mentioned, along shorelines where sea winds move grains up a beach.

Perhaps the least visible form of erosion is from ice moving as large masses called glaciers. Actually, it is not the ice that erodes the surface it moves over, but the sediments picked up by the glacier and residing at the bottom.

Glacial erosion occurs where the climate is cold enough for snow to remain all year, enabling glaciers to develop. Most often they are in the highest and northern-most mountain valleys, such as in the Canadian Rockies, the Alps of Europe, and the mountain ranges of Alaska. In addition, ice sheets, or gigantic glaciers over a mile thick, cover the landmasses of Greenland and Antarctica.

Glaciers use rocky material to erode in the same way that streams use bedloads. A glacier creeping down a valley a few inches a day may pluck from its floor loose or weathered rocks and use them to gouge the floor ahead. In addition, the "nose" of a glacier may act as a bulldozer, scraping up whatever loose material lies before it. When the rocks carried at the bottom ice crumble and wear down to dust, the powder may polish rather than scour the surface that the ice overrides. Through plucking, gouging, scouring, and polishing, glaciers have carved deep,

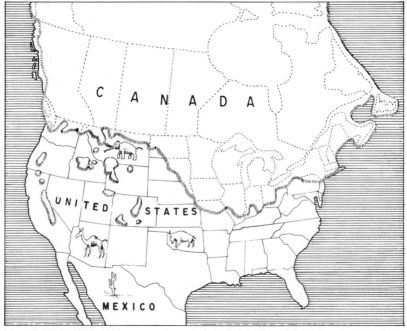

Ice moved across and covered much of North America during the last ice age, reshaping the surface of the continent.

J.C.Holden (from Frozen Earth by R.V.Fodor)

Rock polished by glacial ice in Sequoia National Park, California.

U.S. Geological Survey

U-shaped valleys and jagged peaks in the world's mountain ranges.

Most glacial erosion occurred in the past. The reason is that several times in the last million years, the earth's climate cooled 5 to 6 degrees Celsius. These cool periods, which lasted tens of thousands of years, allowed ice sheets to grow enormously in size and to extend hundreds of miles from the North and South Poles toward the Equator. Midway through these ice ages, ice sheets covered all of Canada and the northern parts of the United States, Europe, and Asia. In mountains such as the Rockies in Colorado and the Sierra Nevadas in California, valley glaciers grew and reached miles farther down their valleys than any surviving glaciers do today.

Because the ice grew mainly from water that came from the oceans, sea level dropped about 300 feet (90 meters) during

Glaciers carved this U-shaped valley in the Sierra Nevadas, California.
Warren Hamilton, U.S.Geological Survey

Glaciers moving across Canada during the last ice age scoured and grooved
this rock surface.   *National Air Photo Library, Canada*

A small glacier spilling out of a valley on Mount Chamberlin, northern Alaska. Moving ice is capable of carving mountain valleys.

U.S. Geological Survey

the ice ages. Seafloor just offshore and now under water was then dry land. Rivers eroding that land account for some of the submarine canyons offshore today. Hudson Canyon, for example, is located offshore from New York and was a 150-foot (45-meter) deep valley for the Hudson River during the last ice age.

Among the features that geologists recognize as evidence of ice ages and the former presence of great erosive glaciers are the U-shaped mountain valleys without glaciers today. Examination of some U-shaped valley floors, such as in Yosemite National Park, California, show the scour and polish marks of glaciers past. Similarly, certain expansive outcrops in Canada and the northern United States contain long glacial grooves that were gouged by rocks in the bottoms of the moving ice sheets.

Elsewhere in Canada and in the Midwestern and

These grass- and tree-covered hills in Canada represent glacial debris, or moraines, left by ice sheets of the last ice age.   *Geology Survey of Canada*

mountainous states there are thick blankets and long ridges of glacial debris. Each of these is called a moraine. They are the glacial erosion products left behind when the ice sheets and mountain glaciers melted. Moraines contain a variety of rock types collected from the many places that the ice passed over.

Of the many kinds of erosion, that from glaciers is least troublesome to humankind. On the other hand, water and wind robbing fertile soil, waves washing away beach property, and landslides crumbling homesites cause financial loss, distress, and even death. To live as comfortably as possible with erosion and to help achieve maximum safety, man has developed several means of protection and prevention. Some work and some do not.

FIGHTING BACK

The cause of a landslide along Interstate Highway 94 near Minneapolis in 1967 puzzled Minnesota highway engineers. Their examination of the region during the construction of the road had not revealed instability in the landscape. With this surprise mass wasting, however, they made immediate plans to reinvestigate the failing slope. The main concern of the engineers was to find the cause and to prevent further sliding.

Obtaining subsurface soil and rock samples was first in order. The investigators drilled fifteen boreholes to collect samples from as deep as 80 feet (25 meters) below the surface. Secondly, they placed scientific instruments, inclinometers and piezometers, into the boreholes.

The purpose of the inclinometers was to measure any changes in inclination, or tilt, of the boreholes. Tilting would mean that there was new horizontal ground movement. The piezometers were to record any changes in the level or in the pore pressure of the groundwater. Aside from gravity, water is the greatest cause of slope instability. Measuring changes in groundwater conditions was therefore critical because increasing

A landslide blocking Highway 24 near Oakland, California.

U.S. Geological Survey

level or pressure may forewarn of additional sliding. Both instruments would help pinpoint where below-the-surface movement was occurring.

A month's research at the Minnesota highway slide located the zone of sliding about 12 feet (4 meters) beneath the lower end of the slope. The investigators dug pits to closely inspect the rock and soil at that depth and discovered sliding taking place on a clay layer only 1 inch (2½ centimeters) thick. When they understood exactly why and where the ground was moving, the engineers ordered concrete buttresses, or supporting props, to be constructed and placed in the slope to halt further sliding.

In Seattle in 1960, excavation for a highway set off movement in a gently sloping sidehill. Engineers for the Washington State Highway Department inspected the area and made inclinometer measurements. The scientific results led them to reestablish slope stability with walls made of thick concrete cylinders planted deep in the slope. Later measurements showed that slope movement had ceased.

Engineers have stopped thousands of landslides by applying modern scientific and construction techniques, and by using concrete and steel. But procedures for stabilizing slopes are always costly and time-consuming. A great amount of money and work-hours could therefore be saved if areas that may possibly slide were recognized and either avoided or modified.

To accomplish this, geologists use a variety of clues and tools. An area with a history of sliding, for example, suggests future mass wasting. Examining aerial photographs—those taken of a region from an airplane—can help detect where slump, earthslides, or rock avalanches already have occurred.

A highway engineer prepares to insert a slope indicator down a bore-hole. *Slope Indicator Company, Seattle*

Construction of this concrete wall will prevent the side hill from slumping onto the highway.　　　　　　*California Department of Transportation*

Any steep slope is a potential slide area, and geologists must visit a region to determine whether or not a hazard exists. They look for signs of rapid creep, such as fence posts sharply tilted or cracked drainage ditches. They consider the amounts of rainfall and vegetation on the slope because abundant rain and little or no plant cover may allow rapid creep.

At the top of a slope, danger signs may be fractures developing from splitting or moving soil cover. A flat area above a slope that has poor drainage is possible trouble. Accumulated rainwater may both weigh heavy on the soil of the slope and lubricate it. One Federal Highway Administration survey revealed that excessive water in soil contributes to 95 percent of all roadside landslides.

Detailed knowledge of rock structure and strength is essential to evaluating slope stability. The dipping of bedding

An ancient slide (center; cross section of slumped rock) is often an indicator of unstable land that may slide again in the future.

U.S. Geological Survey

planes in a rock formation and severe jointing and weathering encourage sliding. And geologists recognize, too, that where a stream or sea waves undercut a steep slope, a landslide is almost assured.

When a field examination indicates a possible hazard, geologists and engineers make special studies. They may dig pits into a slope to see the quality of the earth beneath the surface. Laboratory experiments on the soil and rock will help determine the strength of the slope and its susceptibility to failure. Inclinometers can be set up to determine if movement is underway.

If field and laboratory examinations suggest that a region needed for industrial, residential, or highway construction could possibly slide, retaining walls may be constructed to stabilize the slope. Where falling rocks present a highway danger, a catch fence or wall can be placed along the roadside. If poor drainage threatens to cause a slide, ditches may be dug or pipelines installed to relieve the land of excess water. In some areas the precaution against sliding is to reshape the landscape with machinery that reduces the slope.

Years of erosion reduced the beach at Miami Beach, Florida, to a thin strip (top photo). The Army Corps of Engineers rebuilt the beach to over 300 feet wide (bottom photo; taken 1981).

Army Corps of Engineers,
Jacksonville District

Reshaping landforms has been the prescription for erosion along several shorelines. Where the size and condition of a beach is important for tourism, sand may be added to an eroding beach to rebuild it. Miami Beach, Florida, is one popular vacation spot renourished in this way. After fifty years of hotel development and beach erosion, Miami Beach had been left with only a thin, unattractive strip of bathing beach by the 1960s. Tourists visiting the famous "playground" were both surprised and disappointed about the meager beach. Florida's tourist industry began to drop off.

Using taxpayers' money, the U.S. Army Corps of Engineers came to the rescue. They offered a massive sand-replenishment program to revive the beach and once again attract millions of visitors every year. From the seafloor 2 miles (3¼ kilometers) offshore, they would pump sand onto the coast to create a new beach 10 miles (16 kilometers) long, 300 feet (90 meters) wide, and with an 11-foot (3½-meter) high dune at the top. The cost would be about 65 million dollars.

The project began in 1977 and by 1980 the "new" Miami Beach was ready to receive and please tourists. But its erosional problems may not be over. Some marine geologists are concerned over the shape of the hole left on the seafloor. It could affect the strength and direction of the waves washing ashore. Other scientists wonder about the quality of the new sand. It is comprised mainly of the skeletons and shells of small marine organisms that lived and died in quiet depths. Their fragile remains may not stand up against pounding surf as well as the hard quartz in the original beach sand.

Beach replenishment does not always cure an eroding beach, as demonstrated by the 3 miles (5 kilometers) of recreational shoreline at Wrightsville Beach, North Carolina. A beach nourishment program began in 1939 when the Army Corps of

Engineers pumped 700,000 cubic yards (about 540,000 cubic meters) of sand onto the beach. Wave erosion, however, continued robbing Wrightsville Beach and the Corps made four more sand replenishments totaling about ½ million cubic yards between 1955 and 1960. Then, with still more erosion, the Corps added nearly 3 million cubic yards of sand in 1965, largely to rebuild the dunes at the upper beach.

Shortly after, the Corps constructed a jetty at Masonboro Inlet, located at the down-current (longshore-current) end of the beach. A jetty is a rock or concrete wall that projects into the water at the opening of an inlet or harbor. Its purpose is to trap sands moving in the longshore current and especially to keep them from clogging a harbor or inlet.

Rebuilding Wrightsville Beach, North Carolina, by pumping sand onto the shore and grading it with heavy equipment.

Army Corps of Engineers, Wilmington, NC District

These rock jetties keep Masonboro inlet, North Carolina, free of sand washing in. *Army Corps of Engineers, Wilmington, NC District*

Since the jetty was constructed, the half of the 3-mile beach closest to the jetty has suffered little or no erosion. But the farther half of the beach is undergoing severe erosion, including elimination of the artificial dunes built in 1965. Measurements in 1980 indicated that of all the sand pumped onto Wrightsville Beach since 1939, waves had washed away enough to cover Central Park of New York City with a 4-foot (1¼-meter) thick layer.

While jetties are reducing or stopping erosion in one area, they may also be creating erosional problems nearby. These are sometimes more disastrous than the shoreline problem that the jetty was built to relieve, as at Tillamook Bay, Oregon.

The resort of Bayocean Park at Tillamook Bay began in 1907 when the T.B. Potter Realty Company of San Francisco announced plans to construct the most attractive vacation spot on the Pacific shores. Business-minded people and vacationers quickly bought over 3000 parcels of property on the finger-like strip of land, or spit, that had the Pacific Ocean on one side and

The progressive destruction of the natatorium at Bay'ocean Park, Oregon,
caused by waves eroding the shoreline over about 20 years' time.

Tillamook County Pioneer Museum

Tillamook Bay on the other. To assure that Bayocean Park attracted tourists, the Potter Company constructed a giant natatorium, or swimming palace, and a luxury hotel with bowling alleys, tennis courts, and a dance hall. Bayocean's high growth and tourism over the next ten years lived up to the expectations of the developers.

Then in 1917 the Army Corps of Engineers constructed a jetty on the coast north of Bayocean spit. It was one mile long, and its purpose was to keep sand from washing into the inlet and interfering with ship traffic to Tillamook Bay. But an unexpected result was that the jetty interfered with the supply of sand being brought to Bayocean beaches by the longshore current. Disaster came quickly.

Each year from 1 to 6 feet (1/3 to 2 meters) of the dunes on Bayocean's beaches eroded away. By 1932, the sidewalk alongside the natatorium washed out, and four years later the building collapsed. The hotel fell victim to wave erosion shortly after. Then a 1939 winter storm hurled the final blow at Bayocean. Waves sliced directly across the spit to the bay on the opposite side. Bayocean was suddenly an island cut off from Oregon by wave erosion—because a jetty had disturbed the life-line of sand.

Smaller versions of jetties are constructed along some shorelines to halt local beach erosion. These structures are called groins and they are rock, wood, or concrete walls that jut into the water from the shoreline. Like jetties, their purpose is to trap sand moving in the longshore current.

Usually the trapped sand accumulates in pockets on the side of the groin receiving the current. On the opposite, or down-current, side waves carve into the beach because that area no longer receives sand to keep it built up. The alternating zones of sand-accumulation and sand-erosion on a groined beach gives the shoreline a scalloped appearance.

Of most concern is what happens to the open beaches down-current from a set of groins. A large section of beach deprived of its sand supply could become victim to severe wave erosion. Parts of famous Waikiki Beach in Honolulu, Hawaii, for example, have been robbed of their sands and ruined as bathing areas because of the groins that were built up-current.

When the boat owners of Santa Monica, California, requested a harbor in 1933, they accidentally discovered another way to retain sand in a particular area of a beach. They made the harbor by building a breakwater, or offshore wall, parallel to the shoreline. A breakwater receives the force of the incoming waves, and therefore the water behind it, between the wall and beach, is calm and good for docking boats. What the boat owners did not consider, however, was that reducing the wave energy hitting the beach would interrupt the flow of sand in the longshore current. The decrease in the normal wave energy allowed sand to quickly accumulate on the shoreline

A series of rock groins has altered the shape of this Florida coast, giving a once straight shore a scalloped appearance.

Coastal Engineering Archives, University of Florida

The rock breakwater off the Santa Monica, California, shore protects the beach from strong waves. This allows sand to accumulate on the shore behind it to widen the beach.   *Army Corps of Engineers, Los Angeles District*

directly behind the breakwater. This meant less sand reached the beach down-current. Erosional problems soon developed where the sand supply had dwindled. To rebuild that area, sand from the "growing" beach and from the harbor had to be pumped there.

When a beach is disappearing and erosion threatens the property behind it, protective walls can be built directly on the beach. These are called seawalls, bulkheads, or revetments, and they can be made of steel, concrete, wood, or plastic. Galveston residents, for example, have used a concrete seawall to protect part of the city ever since the 1900 hurricane destroyed most of the city. If construction of a wall is too expensive or unsightly, bags of sand can be laid on the beach as a protective cover.

Bags of sand placed on beaches can serve as protection from wave erosion.

R.V.Fodor

Wherever storm waves are prevented from reaching the sands behind a seawall, they are harsher on the beach in front of the wall. The reason is that huge waves normally roll up onto dunes and then draw back the sand across the lower beach to flatten and widen it. As a beach becomes flatter and wider, it absorbs high wave energy during storms better, and its chances of being washed away are lessened. But deprived of the extra back-beach sands, high-energy waves eventually carry off the beach lying before a seawall and leave only a thin strip. Of the original 325 feet (100 meters) of beach in front of the Galveston wall, only a narrow skirt of rubble remains today.

Moreover, seawalls seldom last more than a few years before requiring expensive repairs. Some seawalls have cost more to construct and repair than the values of the properties they protect.

Engineering techniques, then, are not sure cures for beach erosional problems. They may even create new problems. But even with man's mistakes, shoreline erosion accounts for less than 1 percent of all land lost to erosion. This is in strong contrast to inland erosion where soil lost to running water and wind accounts for nearly all of the land eroded. Enough land disappears to lower the surface of the United States about 2 inches (5 centimeters) every 1000 years. Surprisingly, half of this erosional rate is due to man's modification of the land through agriculture and construction.

Erosion was not recognized as a serious national problem until 1930. That was when Department of Agriculture soil surveyor, H.H. Bennett, persuaded a committee of the U.S. House of Representatives to provide money for research on soil conservation. It was also the time of the Great Depression when over 10 million people were jobless. Accordingly, the Government used the money largely to give unemployed people

Contour farming is planting in parallel rows where all parts of a row are on the same level of a slope. This farming technique reduces runoff on hillsides. *Soil Conservation Service*

The terraces on this Kansas farmland retain water the day after a 4-inch (10-cm) rainfall. Terraces reduce runoff and allow water to seep into the soil.   *Soil Conservation Service*

jobs protecting and improving farmlands. Much of their work was building terraces, or hillside ridges, that form wide, shallow waterways. These embankments allowed excess water to soak in and also reduced the amount of runoff moving downslope, stripping soil.

When the great dust storms of 1933, 1934, and 1935 began destroying agriculture's heartland, the country took a stronger position against erosion. In 1935, Congress and President Franklin D. Roosevelt established the Soil Conservation Service as part of the Department of Agriculture, making H.H. Bennett the director. Notable in that Congressional act was that soil conservation was no longer to be only temporary work for the unemployed. There was now a lasting effort to prevent the nation from washing and blowing away.

Agricultural specialists began developing conservation practices to use in addition to terracing. Still popular today is contouring, or plowing and planting in parallel rows that are exactly level across a slope. When farmers plow this way, there are no straight furrows. Instead, the furrows wind in, out, and around the farmland hills, but always staying level. Like terracing, contouring helps keep runoff from ripping directly and rapidly downslope.

Even though level furrows stop and hold a great deal of runoff, they may fail during heavy rainfall. Many farmers therefore combine strip cropping with contouring. This conservation method alternates sections of protective grasses or clover with the rows of crops that do little to protect soil, such as corn.

Having grassy covers is also vital to retard wind erosion on farmlands. Row crops such as corn, sorghum, and cotton can help, too, if planted in rows perpendicular to the prevailing wind direction. Also, rows of trees bordering farm acreage reduce wind erosion by decreasing wind velocity.

Rows of willow trees make good breakers against wind erosion.

Soil Conservation Service

Shoreline dunes also need protection from wind. Where natural vegetation is meager, grass can be planted. This is how the National Park Service has preserved dunes at Cape Hatteras National Shoreline, North Carolina.

Among the more recent developments in soil conservation are various state and federal laws that require erosion-control procedures on disturbed lands. For example, sediment traps or basins must be used to capture or slow down excess runoff in mining or construction areas. To preserve soil along new highway cuts, laws require grass reseeding immediately after road construction. And land stripped of vegetation during mining must be reseeded.

Concern is presently growing for the erosional damage caused by drivers of ORV's—off-road vehicles such as dune buggies and jeeps. Studies on the Mojave Desert, California, showed that runoff from rainfall on desert land compacted by ORV's occurs in less than half the time it does on normal

To control erosion, employees of the Consolidation Coal Company hydro-seed (squirting water plus seeds) grass on the earth that was piled up during mining.   *Soil Conservation Service*

When off-road vehicles (ORV's) destroy vegetation on shorelines, wind erosion can destroy the dunes.   *North Carolina State University Seagrant*

desert land. And the runoff is 5 times greater, moving 10 to 20 times more sediment than on normal desert land. To add to the erosional problems, destruction of vegetation by ORV's enables wind to erode more effectively. Accordingly, all states have either passed laws or are in the process of passing laws that restrict ORV's from traveling in certain areas. Indiana's law is among the toughest, restricting ORV's from traveling on state-owned land.

Without question, humankind is determined to reduce erosion wherever it interferes with the comforts of living and the necessity of work, or causes waste. Yet, with streams constantly washing soil and rock to sea, it may seem that the continents are destined to be chiseled down to mere islands. This will never happen, however. Mount Saint Helens volcano in Washington state demonstrated one reason why. Its May 1980 explosion of molten rock added several inches of "new" earth to the surrounding Northwest regions. Continents grow through such volcanism and by mountain building. These geologic processes offset erosion—the carving of the earth's surface by gravity, water, wind, and ice.

Volcanism such as at Mount Saint Helens in May 1980, is one way of replacing the rock that is eroded to sea.   *U.S. Geological Survey*

GLOSSARY

abrasion—the mechanical wearing, grinding, or scraping of a rock surface by the rock particles moving over it.

acid rain—rain water containing industrial pollutants from the atmosphere, such as carbon dioxide and sulfur.

alluvial fan—a fan-shaped accumulation of sand, pebbles, and rocks deposited by a stream at the base of a mountain from which it exits. Alluvial fans usually form in dry or desert climates.

avalanche—a swift fall of a large mass of rock, ice, or snow down a mountainside.

base level—the lowest point to which streams can erode, determined by the level of a lake or ocean into which the water flows.

bedload—the sand and rock that moves along the bottom of a stream by rolling and bouncing.

bedding plane—a surface that parallels the sediment layers in a sedimentary rock formation.

blowout—a shallow circular or near-circular depression carved in dry soil or sand by wind erosion.

breakwater—a rock or concrete wall built offshore and parallel to a shoreline to protect the shore from wave erosion.

bulkhead—a wall built on a beach to protect it from wave erosion.

chemical weathering—the breakdown of rocks and minerals by chemical reactions, usually involving rainwater, groundwater, and water in the atmosphere.

contouring—in farming on sloping land, plowing and planting in level rows.

creep—the slow movement of soil and loose rock downslope.

debris flow—a watery mass-movement in which more than half of the solid material is greater in size than sand particles.

delta—an accumulation of mud and sand deposited by a river in a lake or sea near the mouth of the river.

desert pavement—a thin layer of wind-polished stones covering a desert floor.

dissolution—the process of dissolving, such as the chemical weathering of limestone.

dune—a mound of sand deposited and formed by wind.

Dust Bowl—the portion of the Midwest (parts of Oklahoma, Kansas, Colorado, New Mexico, Texas) that suffered great wind erosion in the 1930's.

earthflow—a mass movement of earth detached from a slope and moving in a stream or tongue-like form.

erosion—the loosening and breaking down of rocks and minerals, and their removal downslope, downstream, or downwind.

exfoliation—physical weathering whereby sheets of rock are detached from the underlying rock.

frost heaving—the lifting of surface materials due to the freezing of water beneath them.

glacier—a large mass of ice moving downslope.

groin—a rock or concrete wall projecting in the water from a shoreline.

groundwater—water beneath the surface, usually in the pore spaces of rocks and soil.

hydrologic cycle—the cycle of the earth's water, mainly from ocean to atmosphere to rainfall to streams and then back to sea.

hydrolysis—a chemical weathering process that alters minerals by reaction with water and acids.

jetty—a rock or concrete wall that juts into the water at the opening of an inlet or harbor.

joint—a fracture in a large rock body along which no movement has taken place.

karst—landscape characterized by numerous sinkholes and caves.

landslide—a relatively rapid downslope movement of rock and soil.

longshore current—a current moving along a coast, parallel to the shoreline.

mass movement—the downslope movement of relatively large amounts of rock and soil.

mass wasting—see mass movement.

mechanical weathering—weathering by physical processes such as the expansion of rocks caused by the freezing of water in cracks.

moraine—a large accumulation of rock and soil deposited by a glacier.

mudflow—a relatively rapid mass-movement of mainly mud and sand and having a high water content.

mudslide—a general term for a downslope mass-movement of rock and soil that is somewhat lubricated by water.

physical weathering—see mechanical weathering.

pothole—a hole in the rock bed of a stream carved by abrasion from small particles in a strong current.

quick clay—clay with high water content, that becomes fluid when jarred or shaken.

revetment—a wall built on a beach to prctect it from erosion.

rock avalanche—a rapid slide of a large amount of rock.

rock fall—free-falling movement of rock from a cliff or steep slope.

runoff—rainwater running off the surface.

saltation—the movement of rock particles by bouncing, such as along a stream bed or desert floor.

sediment—rock particles such as sand and mud, carried by water or wind.

sinkhole—a pit or hole in the landscape often caused by the dissolution of limestone or collapse of a cave roof.

slump—the downslope movement of rock and soil as a unit, leaving a spoon-shaped scar on the slope.

spall—the fracturing of rock into sheets.

spheroidal weathering—the weathering of rock whereby spherical boulders are left as layers of the rock flake off.

strip cropping—in farming, alternating protective grasses with crops that do little to protect soil, such as corn.

terracing—in farming, plowing furrows and ridges that form shallow waterways to trap and channel runoff.

ventifact—a rock polished and faceted by wind erosion.

weathering—the disintegration and decomposition of rocks and minerals.

INDEX

DATE		
fac		
fac		
fac		
JAN		
JAN 26		